Comparative Ethnology Of The European And North American Ants

William Morton Wheeler

In the interest of creating a more extensive selection of rare historical book reprints, we have chosen to reproduce this title even though it may possibly have occasional imperfections such as missing and blurred pages, missing text, poor pictures, markings, dark backgrounds and other reproduction issues beyond our control. Because this work is culturally important, we have made it available as a part of our commitment to protecting, preserving and promoting the world's literature. Thank you for your understanding.

Comparative Ethology of the European and North American Ants.

By

William Morton Wheeler,
Harvard University.

(Mit Tafel 3 u. 4 und 6 Textfiguren.)

Eight years ago Professor Forel published a series of observations which he made on the North American ants while on a journey from Toronto, Canada, through Massachusetts and the District of Columbia to the Black Mountains of North Carolina[1]). These observations are of unusual interest to the student of the North American fauna because they were recorded by one thoroughly acquainted with the European species, and one whose unusual powers of observation have rarely missed the essential in the objects of his investigation. For the territory which he covered the comparison he draws between the European and American species is remarkably accurate. But North America comprises an enormous and diversified area, and many of the species observed by the eminent myrmecologist extend their range into territory very unlike that in which he sojourned. As my study of the ants for several years had been confined to North America, I was glad to have an opportunity during the summer of 1907 of visiting Europe and of forming my own impressions of the fauna of that continent. When requested by Dr. Cécile Vogt to contribute to this Festschrift, it seemed appropriate to revert to these impressions, especially as I am under lasting obligations to Professor Forel for leading me at once to an intimate acquaintance with the Swiss species. The circumstances under which I developed this acquaintance were full of the delight of companionship with a genial and inspiring personality, and the emotional appeal which Europe, the mother country of our race, always makes to the American. And if the American happens to be a naturalist, this appeal is wonderfully enhanced. No one can remain unaffected by the monuments of a great civilization, but it is certain that none of these can give the kind of pleasure which the naturalist feels on first hearing the sky-lark or the nightingale, or on first beholding an alpine meadow flooded with gentians or the great colonies of the fallow ants among the pines.

---

[1]) Ebauche sur les moeurs des fourmis de l Amérique du Nord. Rivist. Sci. Biol. n. 3. vol. II, 1900, 13 pp.; translated by A. P. Morse in Psyche IX, 1901, pp. 231—239, II, ibid. pp. 243—245; originally published by Forel as "Lettre de Faisons". Ann. Soc. Entom. Belg. XLIII, 1899, pp. 438—447.

Before presenting my impressions of the European ants, it will be advisable to give a brief sketch of my journey. After leaving New York City May 9, my steamer stopped for a few hours at Ponta Delgada in the Azores (May 16), and then proceeded to Gilbraltar (May 19) and Genoa (May 25). In each of these localities I was able to make a hurried collection of ants. At Ponta Delgada *Lasius niger*, *Tetramorium cæspitum*, and *Ponera eduardi*, three well-known European species, and *Monomorium carbonarium*, probably imported from Madeira, were the only ants found. In the Alameda at Gibraltar *Aphænogaster testaceopilosa* and *Monomorium salomonis*, both of which construct crater nests, were almost the only species observed. The former collects small fallen flowers, leaves and dead insects and carries them into its burrows. At one nest I saw fully a quarter of a litre of dead flowers dumped on the refuse heap near the entrance. Among the hills surrounding Genoa I found two other well-known Mediterranean ants, the harvester, *Messor barbarus*, and *Pheidole pallidula*.

From Genoa I proceeded at once to Professor Forel who was then residing at Chigny on the shores of Lake Leman. This portion of Switzerland is classic ground for the myrmecologist, for it was at Geneva that J. P. Huber pursued his famous "Recherches sur les Moeurs des Fourmis Indigènes" and at Vaud that Forel, as a mere lad, made the observations embodied in his splendid "Fourmis de la Suisse". Here, too, another eminent myrmecologist, Professor Carlo Emery, took up the study of Formicidæ. Certainly I could not have selected a better spot in which to become acquainted with the European species. Although Professor Forel was busy with preparations for moving his household to Yvorne and was weighted down with much other work, he nevertheless welcomed me into the bosom of his charming family and found time to conduct me to the favorite collecting grounds of his youth, the meadows of Vaud and the Petit Salève near Geneva. He also directed me to the most favorable localities in the Jura, Canton Vallais (Fully, Sierre and Sion), Canton Ticino (Monte Generoso and Monte Ceneri) and the Grisons (Upper Engadin). These and several other localities I visited during June. During July I stopped to see my former teacher, Professor Boveri at Würzburg, where I had an opportunity to make a couple of myrmecological excursions with Professors Hans Spemann and K. B. Lehmann. From Würzburg I proceeded to Dresden to see my university chum Professor Escherich, now at the Royal Academy of Forestry at Tharandt. He and Mr. H. Viehmeyer conducted me to the fine collecting grounds in the Dresden heath, where the latter gentlemen has been making many valuable observations on ants. At this point my collecting trips ended as I had to devote some time to the study of the natural history museums of Berlin, Hamburg, Bremen and Altona, before returning to the United States.

I. The Composition of the European and North American Ant-faunas.

The ants, both in Europe and North America, exhibit a mixture of boreal and tropical species. The latter have a very different complexion on the two continents, but the former, the paleoboreal and neoboreal forms with which we are especially concerned, are so closely related as to constitute a single fauna, the holarctic, or circumpolar, and as such range also through temperate Asia. The unitary character of this fauna is evident from the fact that many of the species completely girdle the northern hemisphere, departing so slightly from their specific types on the different continents as to be regarded merely as subspecies or varieties. I shall not discuss the north Asiatic fauna, as it is still very imperfectly known and as I am acquainted with few of the species except those occuring in Japan. The fauna of Europe and America north of Mexico may be properly compared since, although the former country is only about half as large as the latter, there are very few species in British America and Alaska not known to occur in the United States. The latter area is, moreover, smaller than that of Europe.

The following conspectus of a number of palearctic forms and their nearctic representatives in parallel columns shows the close relationship between the two series:

Palearctic	*Nearctic*
Ponerinæ	Ponerinæ
Ponera coarctata Latr.	subsp. *pennsylvanica* Buckley.
Stigmatomma denticulatum Roger.	*S. pallipes* Haldem.
Sysphincta europæa Forel.	*S. mellina* Roger.
Myrmecinæ	Myrmecinæ
Myrmecina graminicola Latr.	subsp. *americana* Emery.
Solenopsis fugax Latr.	*S. molesta* Say.
Cremastogaster scutellaris Oliv.	*C. lineolata* Say.
Myrmica rubida Latr.	*M. mutica* Emery.
M. rubra L. subsp. *sulcinodis* Nyl.	subsp. *brevinodis* Emery.
subsp. *laevinodis* Nyl.	var. *bruesi* Wheeler.
subsp. *scabrinodis* Nyl.	var. *sabuleti* Meinert.
Leptothorax acervorum Fabr.	subsp. *canadensis* Prov.
L. muscorum Nyl.	var. *sordidus* Wheeler.
Harpagoxenus sublævis Mayr.	*H. americanus* Emery.
Stenamma westwoodi Westw.	*S. nearcticum* Mayr.
Aphænogaster subterranea Latr.	var. *occidentalis* Emery.
Messor barbarus L.	*M. pergandei* André.
Dolichoderinæ	Dolichoderinæ
Tapinoma erraticum Latr.	*T. sessile* Say.
Liometopum microcephalum Panz.	*L. apiculatum* Mayr.
Dolichoderus 4-punctatus L.	*D. mariæ* Forel.
Camponotinæ	Camponotinæ
Lasius flavus L.	subsp. *nearcticus* Wheeler.
L. umbratus Nyl.	var. *aphidicola* Walsh.
L. niger L.	var. *neoniger* Emery.
subsp. *alienus* Först.	var. *americanus* Emery.
Formica sanguinea L.	subsp. *rubicunda* Emery.
F. exsecta Nyl.	*F. exsectoides* Forel.
F. rufa L. subsp. *pratensis* De Geer	subsp. *obscuripes* Forel.
subsp. *truncicola* Nyl.	subsp. *integra* Nyl.
F. fusca L.	var. *subsericea* Say.
subsp. *rufibarbis* Fabr.	var. *occidentalis* Wheeler.
F. cinerea Mayr.	var. *neocinerea* Wheeler.
Polyergus rufescens Latr.	subsp. *breviceps* Emery.
Camponotus herculeanus L.	var. *whymperi* Forel.
subsp. *ligniperdus* L.	var. *novæboracensis* Fitch.
C. vagus Scop.	*C. lævigatus* F. Smith.
C. fallax Nyl.	var. *nearcticus* Emery.

The two series of species here enumerated, are the back-bone, so to speak, of the ant fauna in the temperate portions of the two continents and point unmistakably to an ancient common stock in preglacial times. The list also shows another peculiarity which is brought out by dividing the North American species into three groups: those confined to the eastern portion of the continent, those confined to the western portion and those common to both regions. The purely eastern forms in the foregoing representative list number only eight: *Ponera pennsylvanica, Sysphincta mellina, Myrmica bruesi, Harpagoxenus americanus, Dolichoderus mariae, Lasius nearcticus, Formica integra, Camponotus novaboracensis*. The exclusively western forms are ten in number: *Myrmica mutica, Stenamma nearcticum, Aphaenogaster occidentalis, Messor pergandei, Liometopum apiculatum, Formica obscuripes, F. occidentalis, F. neocinerea, Polyergus breviceps, Camponotus laevigatus*. The remaining seventeen forms, or nearly half the total number, extend across the continent. As in so many other groups of animals the balance of the evidence is in favor of a migration of forms from Eurasia by way of Alaska rather than by way of Greenland. In none of the cases above recorded can there be a question of importation by human agencies. The only ant introduced from Europe seems to be *Tetramorium caespitum*, which is confined to the Eastern States. The feeble and sporadic development of its colonies shows that it has difficulty in establishing itself.

When the complete lists of the North American and European ants are compared, some interesting differences are revealed. As these lists are too voluminous to reproduce in the present paper, I shall confine myself to a single genus and a few general statements. Emery and Forel[1]) in 1879 gave the total number of species, subspecies and varieties of European ants as 189, belonging to 37 genera. Ern. André[2]) cites only 120 European forms belonging to 36 genera and subgenera. Although several forms have been since discovered, the present number can hardly exceed 200. For America north of Mexico I have a list of 450 described species, subspecies and varieties, belonging to 63 genera and subgenera. But as a number of forms remain to be described, the total number will probably exceed 500. It is certain, at any rate, that the North American ant-fauna is more than twice as rich as that of Europe and represents nearly twice as many genera and subgenera. Indeed, the nearctic fauna will probably be found to equal or even to surpass that of temperate Europe and Asia combined.

Closer examination shows that, although the greater number of generic and subgeneric types in the North American fauna is due to its larger subtropical component, the boreal component is also proportionally richer than that of Europe. In order to illustrate this statment I give the following complete table of *Formica*, including also the Asiatic forms (in parentheses):

Palearctic Formicae.	*Nearctic Formicae.*
Group *sanguinea*.	Group *sanguinea*.
F. *sanguinea* Latr.; var. *mollesonae* Ruzs.; (var. *fusciceps* Emery). (F. *adelungi* Forel).	subsp. *rubicunda* Emery; var. *subintegra* Emery; var. *subnuda* Emery; subsp. *puberula* Emery; subsp. ob-

---
[1]) Catalogue des Formicides d'Europe. Mitt. schweiz. entom. Gesell. V, no. 8. 1879, pp. 441—481.
[2]) Species des Hyménoptères d'Europe et d'Algérie II. 1881, p. 105.

Group *rufa*.

F. *rufa* L.; var. *meridionalis* Nass.; subsp. *truncicola* Nyl.; (var. *yessensis* Forel); subsp. *pratensis* De Geer.
F. *uralensis* Ruzsky.

Group *exsecta*.

F. *exsecta* Nyl.; var. *rubens* Forel; subsp. *pressilabris* Forel; var. *rufomaculata* Ruzsky; subsp. *etrusca* Emery; subsp. *suecica* Adlerz.

Group *fusca*.

F. *fusca* L.; var. *glebaria* Nyl.; var. *rubescens* Forel (var. *fuscorufibarbis* Forel; var. *nipponensis* Forel); var.

tusopilosa Emery; subsp. *aserva* Forel.
F. *pergandei* Emery.
F. *munda* Wheeler.

Group *rufa*.

subsp. *obscuriventris* Mayr; var. *integroides* Emery; var. *gymnomma* Wheeler; var. *rubiginosa* Emery; var. *melanotica* Emery; subsp. *obscuripes* Forel; var. *whymperi* Forel; subsp. *integra* Nyl.; var. *hæmorrhoidalis* Emery; var. *coloradensis* Wheeler.
F. *moki* Wheeler.
F. *adamsi* Wheeler.
F. *morsei* Wheeler.
F. *oreas* Wheeler.
F. *ciliata* Mayr.
F. *crinita* Wheeler.
F. *dakotensis* Emery.
F. *specularis* Emery.
F. *rufiventris* Emery.

Group *microgyna*.

F. *difficilis* Emery; var. *consocians* Wheeler.
F. *microgyna* Wheeler; var. *rasilis* Wheeler.
F. *nevadensis* Wheeler.
F. *impexa* Wheeler.
F. *nepticula* Wheeler.

Group *exsecta*.

F. *exsectoides* Forel; subsp. *opaciventris* Emery.
F. *ulkei* Emery.

Group *pallide-fulva*.

F. *pallide-fulva* Latr.; var. *succinea* Wheeler; subsp. *schaufussi* Mayr; var. *incerta* Emery; var. *meridionalis* Wheeler; subsp. *nitidiventris* Emery; var. *fuscata* Emery.

Group *fusca*.

var. *subsericea* Say; var. *argentata* Wheeler; var. *densiventris* Viereck; var. *subænescens* Emery; var. *gla-*

gagatoides Rusz.; subsp. *gagates* Latr. *var. filcfmeri Forel* (var. *muralewiczi* Ruzsk.; subsp. *transcaucasica* Nass.); subsp. *subrufa* Roger; subsp. *rufibarbis* Fabr.; var. *glauca* Ruzsky; var. *subpilosa* Ruzsky; subsp. *clara* Forel (var. *caucasica* Ruzsky).

F. *cinerea* Mayr; var. *imitans* Ruzsky; var. *armenica* Ruzsky.

Subgenus *Proformica*.
F. *aberrans* Mayr.
F. *nasuta* Nyl.
F. *krausi* Forel.

cialis Wheeler; var. *neorufibarbis* Emery; var. *neoclara* Emery; var. *gnava* Buckley; var. *occidentalis* Wheeler.

subsp. *subpolita* Mayr; var. *neogagates* Emery; var. *montana* Emery; var. *perpilosa* Wheeler; subsp. *lasioides* Emery; var. *picea* Emery.
var. *neocinerea* Wheeler.
F. *pilicornis* Emery.

This list comprises 29 forms from Europe and 61 from North America. It will also be seen that the *sanguinea*, *rufa* and *fusca* groups are represented by many forms in North America and that the *pallide-fulva* group is confined to this continent. The *exsecta* group seems to be more highly developed in Europe, but it is probable that *F. exsectoides* of the United States embraces several undescribed varieties. The subgenus *Proformica* is not known to occur in the New World. An enumeration of the species, subspecies and varieties of *Polyergus*, *Lasius*, *Myrmica*, *Leptothorax*, *Stenamma*, *Aphænogaster*, *Cremastogaster*, *Solenopsis*, and many other genera common to both hemispheres would give much the same results as *Formica*, showing that the American ants are either affected with a much higher degree of variability or that the conditions for the survival of different forms have been much more favorable. Before we can accept either of these alternatives, it will be necessary to discuss the past history of the ant-faunas on the two continents and the habits of several of the existing species.

II. Ants of the Tertiary and Quaternary Formations.

Although representatives of both the higher and lower groups of Hymenoptera are known from the Mesozoic, Handlirsch[1]) has recently shown that none of them can be assigned to the Formicidæ. According to this authority, the fossils known as *Palæomyrmex prodromus* Heer, *Formicium brodei* Westwood and *Myrmicium heeri* Westwood are not ants, but the first a Homopteron and the two others allied to the horntails (*Sirex*). We must assume, nevertheless, that ants existed during Mesozoic times (in the Trias, or even in the Lias), because in the early Tertiary of Europe the family appears full-fledged and represented by a great number of genera and species. Many of these genera have survived to the present day and even the extinct types are readily referable to existing subfamilies and to no others. The

---

[1]) Die Fossilen Insekten und die Phylogenie der Rezenten Formen. Leipzig. Wilh. Engelmann. 1906—1908.

ants of these extinct groups, moreover, are of such a character that one would not be in the least surprised to find any of them living at the present time in some unexplored portion of the tropics. Among these Tertiary ants the male, female and worker phases were as sharply differentiated as they are to-day. Jos. LeConte[1]) is therefore mistaken when, from the fact that nearly all the fossil ants of Oeningen and Radoboj are males and females, he infers that "the wingless condition, the neutral condition, the wonderful instincts and organized social habits, have been developed together *since the Miocene* epoch". I shall show presently that had he consulted Heer's work[2]) on these insects he could not have fallen into this blunder.

Tertiary ants have been found both in Europe and North America in some 24 localities, representing several geological periods and formations. The following are the European formations: Baltic amber, beds of Aix in the Provence and Gurnet Bay, Isle of Wight (Lower Oligocene); Schoßnitz in Silesia, Krottensee in Bohemia and Rott in the Rhinelands (Upper Oligocene); Radoboj in Croatia, Falkenau and Kutschlin in Bohemia and Cape Staratschin, Spitzbergen (Lower Miocene); Sicilian amber and the beds of Brunnstatt in Alsacia (Middle Miocene); Oeningen in Baden, Parschlug in Styria, Tallya in Hungary, Gabbro in Italy and Thalheim in Transylvania (Upper Miocene); Sinigallia in Italy, Freck, near Hermannstadt, Transylvania (Pleiocene). The age of the North American deposits has not been accurately determined. Ants have been seen in the amber of Nantucket (Goldsmith) which is attributed to the Tertiary. Other localities are Green River, Wyoming; White River, Colorado and Quesnel, British Columbia, which are referred to the Oligocene, and Florissant, Colorado, which is said to belong to the Miocene.

The Baltic and Sicilian amber and the beds of Radoboj, Oeningen and Florissant have yielded far and away the greatest number of ants. The most beautiful specimens are those of the amber, which are often so perfectly preserved that they may be as readily studied as recent ants mounted in Canada balsam. Most of these specimens are workers and belong to more or less aboreal species, but there are also quite a number of males and females. As nearly all of the latter have wings they must have been caught in the liquid resin just before or after their nuptial flight. The preservation of the Oeningen, Radoboj and Florissant specimens is very inferior to that of the amber. The deposits in these localities are lacustrine, that is, they consist of fine sand or volanic ashes laid down in fresh water lakes. This accounts for the fact that nearly all the specimens are males and females, for as Heer says: "with few exceptions only winged individuals are found, because the wingless individuals, in this case the workers, were drowned less frequently than the others. Both males and females occur, but the former are much rarer than the latter, probably because the females, having a much larger and heavier abdomen, fell into the water more often than the males." The fossil ants of Florissant show the same peculiarities, except that the males are not much rarer than the females. Thus the condition which Le Conte interpreted as indicating an absence of the

---

[1]) Elements of Geology. p. 511.

[2]) Die Insektenfauna der Tertiärgebilde von Oeningen und Radoboj in Kroatien. Neue Denkschr. Allgem. Schweiz. Ges. Naturw. 1849, pp. 1—264.

worker caste during Miocene and premiocene times, is easily and naturally explained. It is strange that he failed to see this, especially as in the paragraph immediately preceding the remark above quoted, he calls attention to the following interesting resemblance between modern lacustrine conditions and those which must have prevailed at Oeningen: "On Lake Superior, at Eagle Harbor, in the summer of 1844, we saw the white sands of the beach blackened with the bodies of many species (of insects), but mostly beetles, cast ashore. As many species were here collected in a few days, by Dr. J. L. Le Conte, as could have been collected in as many months in any other place. The insects seem to have flown over the surface of the lake; to have been beaten down by winds and drowned, and then slowly carried shoreward and accumulated in this harbor, and finally cast ashore by winds and waves. Doubtless at Oeningen, in Miocene times, there was an extensive lake surrounded by dense forests; and the insects drowned in its waters, and the leaves strewed by winds on its surface, were cast ashore by its waves."

The conditions described by Le Conte for Lake Superior are common to all our Great Lakes. The insects drowned in them are often buried in the sand of the beaches and might eventually fossilize, but the Tertiary lakes of Oeningen, Radoboj and Florissant must have been much smaller, shallower and calmer bodies of water, and the insects that dropped into them or were swept into them by streams, were probably imbedded in the mud under water. Many of them were, of course, devoured by fishes. Prof. Cockerell has sent me from Florissant several specimens of fossil fish excrement consisting almost entirely of the hard, indigestible heads of ants. It is very unfortunate for the student that so few of the workers of the Oeningen, Radoboj and Florissant ants have been preserved, for our knowledge of ants is largely based on the worker caste, and the males and females even of recent forms, are so imperfectly known that fossils of these sexes are very difficult to classify, especially when the characters of most taxonomic value, such as the shape of the head, mouth-parts and abdominal pedicel, are destroyed by flattening and distortion. Another great difficulty is encountered in attempting to correlate the males, females and workers of the same species. This is no easy task with carelessly collected recent ants, but with fossils, except those of the amber, it becomes almost impossible.

The ants of Oeningen and Radoboj were first studied by Heer[1]) before the taxonomy of recent ants had been placed on a firm basis by the researches of Mayr. It is therefore impossible to assign most of Heer's species to their proper genera, and although Mayr[2]) was able to examine a number of the Swiss paleontologist's species, he did not have access to the types. Hence the whole ant-fauna of Oeningen and Radoboj must be reinvestigated by some one thoroughly acquainted with the recent ants. The species of the Baltic amber have been studied in a masterly manner by Mayr[3]). A few additional species from the same formation were subsequently

---

[1]) Loco citato; Fossile Hymenopteren aus Oeningen und Radoboj. Neue Denkschr. Allgem. Schweiz. Ges. Naturw. 1867, pp. 1—42, 3 pll.

[2]) Vorläufige Studien über die Radaboj-Formiciden. Jahrb. K. K. geolog. Reichsan. XVII, 1867, pp. 47—62, 1 pl.

[3]) Die Ameisen des baltischen Bernsteins. Beitr. Naturk. Preußens I. Königl. phys. ök. Gesell. Königsberg, 1868, 102 pp., 5 pll.

described by Ern. André[1]) and Emery[2]), and the latter has also described 14 species from the Sicilian amber[3]).

According to Handlirsch, of the 600 species of Hymenoptera that have been described from the Tertiary, more than half (307), are ants. These insects must therefore have been very numerous in individuals, just as they are to-day. This is true alike of the Baltic amber and the shales of Raboboj, Oeningen and Florissant. Mayr examined 1460 ants from the amber, Ern. André 698, and through the kindness of Professor R. Klebs of the Royal Amber Museum of Königsberg, and Professor A. Tornquist of the University of the same city, I have been able to examine more than 6000 of these beautiful fossils. Heer says: "The ants are among the commonest fossil animals of Oeningen and Radoboj. In the latter locality they predominate even more in proportion to the other insects than they do at Oeningen. Altogether I have examined 301 specimens, representing 64 species; from Oeningen 151 specimens of 30 species, from Radoboj 143 specimens of 37 species and from Parschlug 7 specimens belonging to 4 species." According to Scudder[4]), "the ants are the most numerous of all insects at Florissant, comprising, perhaps a fourth of all the specimens; they form more than three-fourths, perhaps four-fifths of all the Hymenoptera; I have already about four thousand specimens of perhaps fifty species (very likely many more); they are mostly Formicidæ, but there are not a few Myrmicidæ and some Poneridæ." I have recently made a rapid preliminary study of the 4000 specimens of the Scudder collection belonging to the Museum of Comparative Zoology, and some 3000 more found at Florissant by Prof. T. D. A. and Mrs. W. P. Cockerell, S. Rohwer and myself, and am able to confirm Scudder's statement. There are probably not more than 50 species in both collections, many of them being represented by a great number of specimens. Hardly 70, or one percent, of the 7000 specimens are workers!

Of the Tertiary ants that can be unmistakably assigned to their respective subfamilies, 139 species are Camponotinæ, 25 are Dolichoderinæ, 85 Myrmicinæ, and 27 Ponerinæ according to Handlirsch. A single species (*Anomma rubella*) is referred to the Dorylinæ by F. Smith. I have not seen the description and figure of this insect, but Smith's generic determinations of recent ants were often so erroneous, that his competence to assign a fossil species to its proper genus may be doubted. The proportion of species in the other subfamilies is interesting because it is not unlike that obtaining at the present day except that the Dolichoderinæ are represented by more species. The number of individuals belonging to each subfamily can be satisfactorily given only for the ants of the Baltic amber. Of the 2158 specimens examined by Mayr and André, 764 were Camponotinæ, 1310 Dolichoderinæ, 59 Myrmicinæ and 25 Ponerinæ. The great preponderance of Dolichoderinæ is due to two species, *Bothriomyrmex goepperti* (889 specimens) and *Iridomyrmex geinitzi*

---

[1]) Notice sur les fourmis fossiles de l'ambre de la Baltique et description de deux espèces nouvelles. Bull. Soc. Zool. France XX, 1895, pp. 80—84.

[2]) Deux Fourmis de l'ambre de la Baltique. Bull. Soc. Ent. France, 1905, pp. 187—189, 2 figg.

[3]) Le Formiche dell' Ambra Siciliana nel Museo Mineralogico dell Università di Bologna. Mem. R. Ist. Sci. Bologna, (5) I, 1891, pp. 567—591, 3 pll.

[4]) The Tertiary Insects of North America. U. S. Geol. Survey, Washington, 1890.

(248 specimens). These two ants are therefore represented by 1137 specimens, or more than half of the total number. The species of Myrmicinæ and Ponerinæ are each represented by only a few individuals[1]). From these facts Mayr concludes "that the Ponerinæ of the Tertiary exhibited the weakest development and have reached their full efflorescence in recent times". He advances a similar opinion in regard to the Myrmicinæ. Emery, however, has shown that this inference is erroneous, for the Ponerinæ, — and the same is true of the Myrmicinæ — are much less arboreal in their habits than the Dolichoderinæ and Camponotinæ, and would therefore be much less frequently entrapped in the liquid exudations of the succiniferous trees. Then, too, the Ponerinæ probably formed small colonies as they do at the present time. I have found several undescribed Ponerinæ and Myrmicinæ both in the Baltic amber and in the shales of Florissant, showing that these groups must have been at least as highly diversified in the Miocene and Lower Oligocene as the other two subfamilies.

Only in the amber species have the genera been at all satisfactorily established. Those described from other formations are very largely guesswork. This is especially true of such genera as Heer's *Imhoffia*, *Attopsis* and *Poneropsis*. Other species were placed by him and Scudder in the recent genera *Lasius*, *Formica*, *Dolichoderus*, *Camponotus*, *Myrmica* and *Aphænogaster*, but probably many of these allocations are erroneous. The only genera not represented in the amber but occurring in the Tertiary strata, are *Lonchomyrmex* and *Liometopum*. We may divide the genera of the Baltic and Sicilian ambers into two groups, the extinct and the recent, and the latter may be subdivided into those still represented by species in Europe (palearctic), which are nearly all common to the nearctic region as well (holarctic), and those now confined to the tropics of the Old World (paleotropical). Grouping the genera thus, we have the following table:

Baltic Amber.	*Sicilian Amber.*
1. Extinct Genera.	
Prionomyrmex	*Acrostigma*
Bradyponera	*Hypopomyrmex*
Propodomyrma gen. nov.	
Nothomyrmica gen. nov.	
Electromyrmex gen. nov.	
Stigmomyrmex	
Lampromyrmex	
Enneamerus	
Paraneuretus gen. nov.	
Protaneuretus gen. nov.	
Rhopalomyrmex	
2. Existing Genera.	
a) *Palearctic.*	
Ponera	*Ponera*
Monomorium	*Cremastogaster*

---

[1]) I have not yet completed the statistics of the amber ants which I have examined, but the proportions of the various species are similar to those recorded by Mayr.

Aphænogaster *Tapinoma*
Myrmica *Plagiolepis*
Leptothorax
Dolichoderus
Bothriomyrmex
Tapinoma
Plagiolepis
Prenolepis
Lasius
Formica
Camponotus

b) *Paleotropical.*

Ectatomma *Ectatomma*
? *Anomma* *Aëromyrma*
Sima *Cataulacus*
Oligomyrmex *Leptomyrmex*
Aëromyrma *Technomyrmex*
Cataulacus *Oecophylla*
Iridomyrmex *Gesomyrmex*
Oecophylla
Dimorphomyrmex
Gesomyrmex
? *Polyrhachis*

Of the 40 genera included in this table, 13 are extinct and 27, or more than two thirds, are still living. Of the latter a little more than half (14) are represented in Europe and a little less than half (13) in the Old World tropics. It will also be seen that the ratio (7 : 4) of exclusively paleotropical to palearctic genera in the Sicilian amber is nearly twice that of the Baltic amber (11 : 13), although very few specimens of the former have been examined. But it should be noted that all the palearctic genera enumerated for the Sicilian amber are also common to the paleotropical fauna of the present day. This will explain the following quotation from Emery[1] "My studies on the ants of the Sicilian amber have demonstrated that at the beginning of the Tertiary, Europe had an ant-fauna of Indoaustralian character, still living and exclusively of this character in Sicily during the formation of the amber; while to the north of the sea, which at that time extended across Europe, representatives of this fauna, mingled with *Formica*, *Myrmica* and other recent holarctic types, lived in the forests of the Samland. After the disappearance of this sea the northern fauna pushed its way southward as far as the Mediterranean. Then came the Glacial epoch, which extinguished the Indian fauna in the north and drove its feeble remnants, mingled with arctic forms, to the warmer localities of southern Europe. From these regions the present ant-fauna wandered back, with the disappearance of the ice, into the middle and northern portions of the

---

[1] Beiträge zur Kenntnis der nordamerikanischen Ameisenfauna (Schluß). Zool. Jahrb., Abt. f. Syst. VIII, 1894, pp. 257—360, pl. VIII.

continent. But the tropical forms had difficulty in returning, because the Mediterranean, the African deserts and the steppes to the east were so many obstacles to their progress. The European ant-fauna therefore remains comparatively poor."

In North America, however, notwithstanding the severe glaciation to which the northern portion of the continent was subjected, there was an opportunity for the retreating ant-fauna to return over Mexico and the West Indies, if, indeed, it actually receded further southward than the Gulf States. Many more Tertiary forms, therefore, escaped extinction and this may account for the appearance of greater and more recent variability in North America than in Europe. It is not improbable, however, that a certain amount of this variability is the result of a postglacial migration of the species into new territory.

The mixture of arctic and tropical forms in the amber, a peculiarity which characterizes the other insects and the plants no less than the Formicidæ, has not been satisfactorily explained. Heer[1]) endeavored to account for it on the following assumptions: „It is probable that the succiniferous forests also covered Scandinavia and that the conifers were able to grow on the high mountains. As the amber region extended from Scandinavia to Germany, where a sea separated it from the remainder of the Germanic continent, we may see in this natural barrier the cause of the peculiar facies of the amber flora. It presents to our view the Scandinavian type of the Tertiary, mixed, in all probability, with a mountain type. It is, in fact, conceivable that the plants and animals, embalmed as they were in their elegant amber sarcophagi, could be carried long distances without sustaining the slightest injury and could therefore present this exceptional appearance which is seen nowhere else in the plants and animals of the ancient world. If we suppose that a river flowed down from the Sweden of that day and opened into the Tertiary sea near Danzig, there would be nothing irrational in admitting that this stream might easily carry the amber in the resinous state from the distant localities and mountains of Sweden, so that the organic remains enclosed in the amber may have been gathered together from an extensive territory, from low as well as from mountainous countries, and may even belong to different Tertiary periods. * * * * * If we admit that the amber does not belong to one and the same epoch, we can explain why in the plants and animals of this formation the mixture of northern and southern types is so much more striking than it is in the remainder of the European Tertiary, and why we find among them several types peculiar to high latitudes or even to mountains."

I am unable to accept this view for the following reasons: first, because I have found among the material sent me by Professor Tornquist a single piece of amber containing a tropical *Dolichoderus* wrapped about the body of a *Formica* which is practically indistinguishable from the existing *F. fusca*. This proves, of course, that the two species, which now have their closest allies in India and northern Europe respectively, must have foraged on the same tree trunk during Lower Oligocene times. Second, the fact that the paleotropical species, like the extinct genera of the above table, are represented by very few specimens, compared with the boreal genera, is not easily explained by supposing that a river brought down from Tertiary Scandinavia lowland and mountain forms intermingled and

---

[1]) Recherches sur le Climat et la Végétation du Pays Tertiaire. Trad. C. T. Gaudin. Winterthur, Jean Wurster.

deposited them together in the beds of northern Germany, for on this assumption we should expect to find the lowland or tropical greatly in excess of the boreal specimens. And third, we should hardly expect the succiniferous trees to grow in both tropical and subalpine environments. It is more natural to suppose that during the Lower Oligocene the now extinct tropical species were reduced to dwindling relicts in the Samland, though still coexisting with the boreal types already in possession of the amber forests. In other words, even at that early day, the modern genera were far and away the more vigorous and prolific in the region which was to become their exclusive heritage as soon as the Glacial epoch had wiped out the tropical genera that were leading a precarious existence in the warmer and more sheltered spots. We may assume, therefore, that the greatest development of the tropical genera in this northern region occurred during the Eocene or even during the Mesozoic, and that the adverse climatic conditions which culminated in the Ice Age, were already beginning to have a deadly effect on the older, tropical ants of the Lower Oligocene. The reduction of the once very rich European ant-fauna has therefore been in progress since the early Tertiary, but, as Emery has suggested, the severest blow to this fauna was sustained during the Ice Age.

To these general considerations of the amber fauna a few remarks on some of the more interesting genera and species may be appended:

1. Ponerinæ. — The most conspicuous of these is the large *Prionomyrmex longiceps* of the Baltic amber. This ant is allied to the Australian *Myrmecia*, the most primitive of living Formicidæ, but is even less specialized in the structure of the mandibles and abdominal pedicel. Another interesting but much smaller species is *Bradyponera meieri*, which foreshadows our modern species of *Sysphincta* and *Proceratium*. I have also found in the Baltic amber four new Ponerine genera remotely related to the Indoaustralian *Cerapachys*, *Bothroponera* and *Diacamma*.

2. Myrmicinæ. — Of this subfamily there are several genera which show a wide range of organization and specialization in both the Baltic and Sicilian ambers. *Hypopomyrmex bombiccii*, a singular ant described by Emery from the latter formation, although possessing 10-jointed antennæ and a well-developed venation in the wings, seems to represent a generalized type from which the modern Dacetoni may have sprung. In the Baltic amber *Stigmomyrmex*, with 10-jointed, and *Enneamerus*, with only 9-jointed antennæ, are remarkable forms. The latter, except in the small number of antennal joints, resembles the paleotropical *Pristomyrmex*. Several species referred by Mayr to the genus *Macromischa*, because they lack spurs on the middle and hind tibiæ, do not belong to this genus, which is exclusively neotropical and largely West Indian, but must be placed in a new genus, which may be called *Nothomyrmica*. Much more like the true *Macromischa* than any of Mayr's species, especially in the structure of the thorax and petiole, is an extraordinary ant which I shall describe in a future paper as *Electromyrmex klebsi*. This and many other amber Myrmicinæ are as exquisitely sculptured as any of our modern species. *Propodomyrma* from the Baltic and *Acrostigma* from the Sicilian amber are related to the paleotropical *Podomyrma* and *Atopomyrmex*, but are simpler and more primitive in their structure.

3. Dolichoderinæ. — This subfamily is represented by a number of interesting forms, many of which Mayr originally assembled in the genus *Hypoclinea*. Among

these it is now possible to recognize species of *Dolichoderus, Iridomyrmex* and *Bothromyrmex*. In the material sent me by Professors Klebs and Tornquist there are single specimens of two new genera (*Protaneuretus* and *Paraneuretus*) of unusual interest. Both of these are closely allied to *Aneuretus*, a genus which is now represented by a single species, *A. simoni*, described by Emery from Ceylon. This ant combines both Dolichoderine and Ponerine characters, having the head of the former, and the petiole and sting of the latter subfamily. In the Sicilian amber Emery has recognized a male *Leptomyrmex* (*L. maravignæ*), a genus now confined to Australia and New Guinea, an extremely small *Tapinoma* (*T. minutissimum*) and a *Technomyrmex* (*T. deletus*), another Indomalayan genus. As the Dolichoderinæ are practically absent from the African continent, the great development of this subfamily in the two ambers shows that the complexion of the European Tertiary ant-fauna was decidedly Indoaustralian.

    4. Camponotinæ. — The amber species of *Oecophylla, Gesomyrmex, Dimorphomyrmex* and *Rhopalomyrmex* are worthy of note. *Oecophylla* and *Gesomyrmex* occur both in the Baltic and Sicilian ambers, *Oe. brischkei* and *G. hörnesii* in the former and *Oe. sicula* and *G. cornifer* in the latter. These species of *Oecophylla* are closely related to *Oe. smaragdina*, the well-known red tree ant of the Old World tropics. *Gesomyrmex* was supposed to be an extinct genus till Ern. André described a species (*G. chaperi*) from Borneo[1]. In the same paper and from the same locality he described the type of another interesting Camponotine genus, *Dimorphomyrmex janeti*. This has polymorphic workers with large reniform eyes and 8-jointed antennæ. Some years later (1905) Emery found a species (*D. theryi*) of this same genus in the Baltic amber. *Rhopalomyrmex* resembles the neotropical *Myrmelachista*. It has 10-jointed antennæ, with 4-jointed clubs. Only a few species of the recent genera *Lasius, Formica* and *Camponotus* have been described from the Baltic amber. The workers of one of the *Camponoti, C. constrictus*, are peculiar in possessing ocelli and in having a thorax like *Formica*. Of this latter genus Mayr described only a single species, *F. flori*, which is very closely related to the existing *F. fusca*.

    Our knowledge of the fossil ants of North America is unfortunately very meager. Scudder described *Lasius terreus* and a *Myrmica* sp. from the Green River Oligocene, *Camponotus vetus, Liometopum pingue* from the White River Oligocene and *Formica arcana, Dolichoderus obliteratus* and *Aphænogaster longæva* from the Quesnel formation, but neither the descriptions nor the figures make it at all certain that these ants are assigned to their proper genera. He also described and figured (loc. cit p. 606, pl. III, fig. 32) the wing of an ant as that of a Braconid (*Calyptites antediluvianum*). Cockerell[2] described a *Ponera hendersoni* from the Florissant shales, but the size of the specimen shows that it cannot belong to *Ponera* as at present defined. My preliminary study of the Florissant material shows the presence of many Dolichoderinæ (*Dolichoderus, Liometopum*) and Camponotinæ, large Ponerinæ allied to *Sysphincta* and several Myrmicinæ, one of which resembles *Pogonomyrmex*. The fauna was undoubtedly very rich compared with that now existing in the same locality which has an elevation of over 8000 feet and is therefore subalpine. Both

---

    [1] Voyage de M. Chaper à Bornéo. Catalogue des Fourmis et Description des Espèces Nouvelles. Mém. Soc. Zool. France V., 1892, pp. 46—55, 5 figg.

    [2] A New Fossil Ant. Entom. News, Jan. 1906, pp. 27, 28.

the fossil ants and the other insects, no less than the plants, show that the Miocene climate must have been subtropical like that of the Gulf States at the present time. Although the contrast between the Tertiary and living ants in North America is by no means as great as it is in Europe, it must be remembered that the fauna of Florissant is more recent than that of the Balti camber and more like that of Radoboj and Oeningen. Further statements, however, are premature, since none of these faunas has as yet been carefully studied and compared.

Very few ants are known from the Quaternary, or Pleistocene. Some Camponotinæ and Dolichoderinæ are recorded by Handlirsch as having been found by Benassi in the interglacial deposits of Re, Italy, and Pax[1]) cites a male *Solenopsis fugax* from the Schieferkohle of Freck, near Hermannstadt. These meager data indicate that the Quaternary ant-fauna of Europe was essentially like that now existing. The Quaternary ants of the tropics are more numerous. They are preserved in the copal, an amber-like fossil resin found in several countries (Africa, Brazil, New Zealand, etc.). The earliest account of these ants is that of Blochs[2]) who described and figured specimens of what he called "*Formica saccharivora*", "*salomonis*", "*nigra*" and "*Formica sp.*" In a fine series of copal specimens from Zanzibar in the American Museum of Natural History, I find well-preserved specimens belonging to the following genera: *Camponotus, Polyrhachis, Myrmicaria, Cremastogaster, Pheidole, Cataulacus, Atopomyrmex, Ponera* and *Anomma*, and to species very closely related to, if not identical with, those now living in the same region. In a specimen of copal from Demerara in the same collection there is a worker *Azteca*.

In reviewing the Tertiary and Quaternary ants one is impressed with two facts that have not been sufficiently emphasized in the preceding pages. One of these is the close similarity of some of the ants of the Baltic amber to species now living in the same region. So intimate is this similarity that it may, in a few cases at least, amount to identity, e. g. in *Ponera atavia, Lasius schiefferdeckeri* and *Formica flori*, which neither Mayr nor myself have been able to distinguish by any satisfactory characters from the living *Ponera coarctata, Lasius niger* and *Formica fusca*. Such cases bring home to us very forcibly the enormous age and stability of species which one dealing exclusively with living forms would be inclined to regard as of very recent origin.

The second fact is one to which attention seems not to have been called by previous authors, namely, the absence of polymorphism in the workers of the Tertiary ants. There are, indeed, differences in stature between workers of the same species, and these are sometimes considerable (e. g. in *Bothriomyrmex goepperti*), but I have seen no specimens with sufficient differences in the size and shape of the head to indicate the existence of soldiers and workers proper. This is the more noticeable because there are recorded from the amber several genera whose living species have polymorphic workers, such as *Anomma, Aëromyrma, Oligomyrmex, Camponotus* and *Dimorphomyrmex*. The amber specimens of *Aëromyrma* and *Oligomyrmex* are all males and females, so that nothing is known concerning the

---

[1]) Einige fossile Insekten aus den Karpathen. Zeitschr. f. wiss. Insekt.-Biol. IV, 1908, pp. 99, 100.

[2]) Beitrag zur Naturgeschichte des Kopals. Beschäft. Berl. Gesell. Naturf. Freunde. II, 1776, pp. 91—196, pll. 3—5.

workers, which may have been monomorphic. To the former genus belongs also, according to Emery, the *Pheidologeton antiquus* described by Mayr from a female specimen. The occurrence of *Anomma* in the amber is, as I have said, very doubtful. There remain then only the genera *Camponotus* and *Dimorphomyrmex* in which we might expect to find polymorphic workers. I have examined a number of specimens of the three species of *Camponotus* (*mengei, igneus* and *constrictus*) described by Mayr, but all of them have the form of the minor workers of some of the less polymorphic recent *Camponoti*. *Dimorphomyrmex theryi* was based on a single specimen, but four others which I have seen are monomorphic and in this respect unlike the living type of the genus from Borneo. It may be objected, of course, that no conclusions as to the presence or absence of polymorphism in the workers can be drawn from the amber material, both because it is too meager and because the soldiers do not forage like the workers and would not therefore be liable to be caught in the liquid resin. This is certainly true of some genera, but not of *Camponotus*, to judge from our modern species. The fact remains that no polymorphic workers have been seen in the amber, that the great majority of the species certainly had only monomorphic workers and that genera like *Pheidole* and *Pheidologeton*, so prominent in the Old World tropics to-day, are conspicuous by their absence. In the Pleistocene, however, genera like *Camponotus*, *Pheidole* and *Anomma* have the worker polymorphism fully developed, as I have observed in the Zanzibar copal, so that this condition must have made its appearance during the latter part of the Tertiary.

III. Nidification of the European and North American Ants.

From the foregoing review of our knowledge of the paleontological history of the European and North American ants, we may turn to the habits of the existing species. And since the shape and structure of the nest furnish the most convenient and conspicuous materials for comparative study, we may properly introduce the subject with a quotation from Professor Forel's paper on the North American ants:

"And first, a remark of general character relative to what has surprised me in the highest degree. In North America, with some rare exceptions, the ants do not construct mounds, either of masonry or of other materials.

"In Europe, as you know, ant-hills abound in every meadow, in the woods, in clearings, among the mountains. On coming to a country where the fauna is so similar to that of our own, where so many species only differ from ours in characters often but little distinctive, where the tillage, the fields, the woods, closely resemble those of Europe, I was entirely taken aback when I observed that the varieties of our most common species: *Lasius niger, alienus, flavus, Formica fusca, sanguinea*, etc. do not build any masonry mound, but live in hidden, subterranean nests, opening only under stones or on the ground-level by a little crater. But the fact is the same from Canada to North Carolina. I was forced to submit to the evidence. However, the Americans know what an "ant-hill" is. When conversing with them, they refer to it as a great rarity which can be found in such and such a forest twenty or thirty miles away. And on going there you find a colony of *Formica exsectoides*, the only species in eastern North America which regularly makes large, elevated conical mounds of earth in the forests. I visited two of these colonies in the vicinity of Worcester and of Black Mountain. The nests open by holes situated at the base and about the periphery. The workers do not make excavated roads like our *rufa* of Europe.

"Besides these, *Formica fusca* r. *subsericea* and *pallide-fulva* rarely make small mounds. As for *subsericea*, so common everywhere, I have seen its mounds only at Niagara, at the side of the fall.

"After mature reflection I have come to the conclusion that this singular fact does not seriously weaken my theory of the domes, but rather confirms it. In my "Fourmis de la Suisse", I have shown that the elevated dome is used by our ants to collect and concentrate on their larvæ the radiant solar heat which they so much need, and I cited a number of facts in support of this view. But the climate of North America is entirely different from ours. Extremely cold in winter, it is burning in summer; these are extremes of which we in Europe have no idea. The ants consequently have quite enough heat and sunlight for their larvæ. The dome is superfluous. What they do need is protection from extreme temperatures. For this purpose it is necessary either to mine deeply or to locate themselves in the shade and in the decaying trunks of forest trees. And that is what they do. At least it is in this way that I explain most readily this fact, so surprising by its generality".

If Forel was surprised to find almost no masonry domes in the Eastern United States, my astonishment at their development in the canton of Vaud was equally great. When, early in June, I reached Professor Forel's former residence at Chigny, the long grass in the meadows had not yet been mown, but along the roadsides and on the lawns the number of masonry domes and the diversity of the ants inhabiting them was apparent. When, however, later in the month, the hay had been removed, the number of these peculiar nests could only be regarded as extraordinary. As Forel has shown[1]), they are built by the following ants: *Lasius niger, alienus, flavus, mixtus* and *umbratus, Formica fusca* (including *glebaria* and *rubescens*), *rufibarbis, sanguinea* and *gagates, Camponotus æthiops, lateralis, sylvaticus* and *ligniperdus, Tetramorium cæspitum, Solenopsis fugax, Tapinoma erraticum* and all the subspecies of *Myrmica rubra* (notably *M. lævinodis*). This list includes most of the common ants of temperate Europe.

At this point a brief digression on the different types of ant-nests in temperate regions will help in the further discussion. We may distinguish three types which are constructed for the purpose of utilizing the warmth of the sun's rays in the incubation of the brood:

1. The masonry domes above mentioned. These are earthen structures, usually of small size and often built around the roots or stems of plants, and contain galleries and chambers above the general level of the soil.

2. Accumulations of vegetable detritus (leaves, sticks, grass, etc.) around the entrances of nests in stumps or logs or under stones. Such nests are constructed by many species of *Formica*, especially by *F. truncicola* and *sanguinea* in Europe and *F. integra* and its allies in North America (Figs. 1 and 2).

3. Mound nests, made of vegetable débris and representing a further development of the tendency displayed in nests of the second type. The best examples of the mound nests are furnished by the European *F. rufa* (Fig. 3) and *pratensis* and the North American *obscuripes* (Fig. 4).

---

[1]) Les Fourmis de la Suisse. Zürich, 1874, p. 163.

In addition to these there are four other types of nests:

1. Nests under stones. The stones not only shelter the galleries which extend down into the soil but prevent the soil from drying out. They also become heated with the sun's rays and thus assist in the incubation of the brood.

2. Crater nests. Like the preceding, these nests are mined in the soil, but their entrances are surmounted by earthen craters whose walls are not perforated with galleries or chambers.

3. Nests in logs, stumps, cow-dung, etc., with the galleries extending into the subjacent soil and without accumulations of detritus about the entrances.

4. Nests in plant cavities. These are an essentially tropical type which is rather infrequent in temperate regions.

Nests of all of these forms occur both in North America and Europe and on both continents the same species of ant may greatly modify the structure of its formicary to suit the immediate environment. Forel's remarks above quoted suggest two questions: Are the conditions he observed universal in North America? And how far do the conditions obtaining on that continent support his theory of the masonry domes and mound nests?

It is unquestionably true that the ants of the Eastern United States rarely make masonry domes and do not make mound nests. The striking exception, *Formica exsectoides* (Fig. 5), is, however, much more abundant than Forel supposed. Moreover, the nests of this ant are really hugh masonry domes since it uses earth very largely and but little vegetable detritus in their construction. Hence they resemble the nests of *F. fusca* much more closely than those of *F. rufa* and *pratensis*. It may be rather positively stated that no true mound nests occur in North America east of Illinois and Wisconsin. *F. subsericea* often constructs low, flat, masonry domes in meadows and similar nests are occasionally made by *Lasius aphidicola, claviger*, and *interjectus* and *Myrmica brevinodis* and *detritinodis*. As a rule, however, these ants do not build domes, but nest under stones or in or under old logs or stumps. With nests like those of *F. truncicola* matters are different, for all our eastern forms of the *F. rufa* group, namely, *F. integra, difficilis, consocians, nepticula* and *obscuriventris* make nests of this type. Our forms of *F. sanguinea* show this tendency to accumulate vegetable detritus about the nest entrance less distinctly than the European form or any of the *rufa* series. Our other *Formicæ* live under stones or make obscure crater nests. In this connection an imported species, *Tetramorium cæspitum*, which in Europe often makes masonry domes, is particularly interesting, because in the Eastern States it always nests under stones or makes small crater nests, just as it does in xerothermic localities in Switzerland, Italy and North Africa.

When we leave the Eastern States, however, and travel through the Middle West and thence to the Rocky Mountains we observe a marked change in the nesting habits of many of the North American ants. Even in Western New York, as Forel seems to have observed, *F. subsericea* makes masonry domes and these become larger as we journey through Ohio, Indiana, Illinois and Wisconsin. In these states they are often conspicuous objects in the meadows and along the roads. Here, too, *F. neocinerea* makes its appearance and this and the yellow species of *Lasius* (*aphidicola, claviger, latipes* and *interjectus*) also construct domes. In Illinois and Wisconsin we first meet with a member of the *rufa* group, *F. obscuripes* var. *melanotica*, which makes a true mound nest of small sticks and other vegetable débris, like that of the European *F. pratensis*. Traveling westward through Iowa or Dakota to Colorado, we see the *obscuripes* nests growing larger, more numerous and still more like those of *pratensis*, and as we ascend the foot-hills of the Rocky Mountains we find many of the species of *Formica* making masonry domes, e. g. *F. opaciventris*, which is a subspecies of the eastern *F. exsectoides*, *F. argentata*, representing *F. fusca*, and *F. neocinerea*. There are besides a great number of forms of the *rufa* group, which collect vegetable detritus about stumps, logs and stones, after the manner of *F. truncicola*. But the most abundant and conspicuous nests in this region, at an altitude of 2000 to 2500 m. are those of a Myrmicine ant, *Pogonomyrmex occidentalis* (Fig. 6). These are modified masonry domes of very elegant shape and surrounded by a

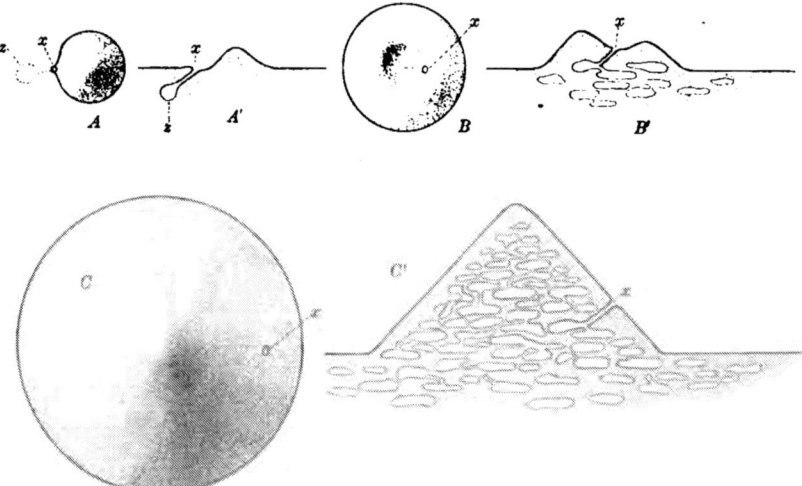

Fig. A. Diagrams of three stages in the development of the modified masonry dome of *Pogonomyrmex occidentalis*. *A*, small mound of earth thrown up by queen when starting her formicary; *x*, entrance, *z*, first chamber; *A'*, same nest in section; *B*, crater nest (second year) formed by incipient colony; *B'*, section of same; *C*, masonry dome of adult colony; *C'*, section of same showing galleries and chambers.

large circular clearing. I have found that they develop from craters. All the other species of *Pogonomyrmex*, except *P. molefaciens* in certain localities, construct crater nests (Fig. 8 and 10) and the incipient nest of *P. occidentalis* is also of this type. With the growth of the colony it is gradually converted from a small crescentic crater into a large earthen and pebbly cone containing many chambers and galleries (**Fig. A**) and with an eccentric, basal entrance almost universally on the south or east side. We see, therefore, that the Rocky Mountain region, notwithstanding its much greater altitude, and much less humid soil and atmosphere, presents conditions not unlike the Alps. The Rocky Mountains, too, as we have seen are also the region, which in the composition of the ant-fauna, is most like the Eurasian continent.

Turning southward now and descending to the lower altitude of the dry, sun-parched deserts of western Texas, New Mexico and Arizona, we fin dthat the ants no longer make masonry domes or mounds, but build craters or live under stones. There is also a marked change in the species, many subtropical forms entering into the fauna. Even *Pognomyrmex barbatus*, which, as the variety *molefaciens* in the moister portions of Eastern Texas, lives in modified masonry domes much like those of *P. occidentalis*, but with a central, apical instead of an eccentric, basal entrance, here makes a very flat vestigial crater or abandons this construction altogether, till its nest is reduced to a circular clearing with a central opening (Fig. 9). The typical form of the species, however, on the high Mexican plateau again resumes the habit of constructing large domes.

How are we to interpret these curious differences in the nesting habits of the ants in different parts of North America in the light of Forel's theory that the domes and mounds are arrangements for utilizing the sun's heat in accelerating the development of the ant brood? This theory is based on certain more general peculiarities in the distribution and structure of the nests, which may be briefly considered before attempting the application of the theory to the diverse conditions described above. That ants are fond of placing their nests in sunny locations is shown by their conspicuous preference for the southern and eastern slopes of hills and mountains. As Forel says: "Another fact to which Blochmann first called attention in Europe in connection with *Camponotus ligniperdus* is the following: The nests of ants abound above all on hill-slopes facing the east. I have confirmed this statement since then many a time, and here in America again. In this case also the explanation seems simple: The morning sun awakens the ants and urges them to work. After noon it is warm enough, they no longer need the sunshine. Hence the advantage of an easterly exposure which provides for a large amount of daily activity. Towards the west, on the contrary, they would lose the first hours of the morning, would be unable to work on account of the heat after noon in summer, and could do next to nothing in the evening to make up for it, once the night was come. Moreover, the night equalizes very quickly the eastern and western exposures so that the latter do not even prolong the afternoon's activity among those species which work at night. Ants, then, have every advantage in securing sunshine in the morning and shade in the afternoon — in America as in Europe."

Muckermann[1]), who resided for several years at Prairie du Chien in southwestern Wisconsin, considered both the position of the ant-nests on slopes and the absence or scarcity of domes and mounds in America. He accepted the latter of Forel's views but failed to observe any preference of the ants for eastern exposures: "For here ant-hills abound on eastern and western slopes alike." It is probable that the hills of southwestern Wisconsin are too low to show very clearly the peculiarity mentioned by Forel. My own observations both in the Litchfield hills of Connecticut and in the mountains of Colorado and New Mexico confirm the Swiss myrmecologist's statements.

Not only are the nests placed on the slopes most favorable for utilizing the sun's heat but the individual nest is often beautifully adapted to this same purpose. The solar orientation of the nests of *Lasius flavus* in the Alps was first described by J. P. Huber[2]). He says: "These same little yellow ants, which possess

---

[1]) The Structure of the Nests of Some North American Species of Formica. Psyche IX, June 1902, pp. 355—360.

[2]) Recherches sur les Moeurs des Fourmis Indigènes. Paris, J. J. Paschoud, 1810, p. 519 nota.

aphids, serve as compasses to the mountaineers when they lose their way in the dense mists, or stray during the night into unfamiliar places; and in this manner: their formicaries which, in the mountains, are much more numerous and much higher than they are elsewhere, take on an elongate and almost regular form. Their direction is constantly from east to west. Their summit and most abrupt slopes are turned toward the winter sunrise, but the opposite side slopes gradually." These nests have been recently observed by Tissot[1]), and I have found the nests of *Formica argentata* shaped and oriented in much the same manner in the subalpine meadows of Florissant, Colorado (altitude 2700 m). Equally striking is the case of *Pogonomyrmex occidentalis*, for the shape of the nest-cone, the materials of which it is built, the arrangement of its galleries and chambers, the almost constant position of the entrance on the south or east side and the carefully cleared area surrounding the whole, are all so many contrivances for utilizing to its fullest extent the sun's heat in hastening the development of the brood and in keeping the seeds, which this ant garners, from germinating.

Granting that there is ample evidence to show that ant colonies build their domes and mounds in the most favorable positions for utilizing the radiant heat of the sun, how are we to account for the almost complete absence of these structures in the Atlantic States, their greater development in the Middle West, their greatest development at an elevation of 2000 to 3000 m. in the Rocky Mountains, and their complete absence in the deserts of the Southwest? I believe that Forel's theory will explain these facts, if we take into consideration the annual percentage of sunshine, the mean annual temperature and the mean annual maximum and minimum temperatures of the regions above cited. Taking our data from the recently published tables of Henry[2]) for New York, Omaha, Denver and Yuma, we find that the annual percentage of sunshine increases as follows: New York City 56%, Omaha 60%, Denver 69%. The percentage for Yuma is not given, but certainly exceeds that of Denver. The annual mean minimum and maximum temperatures show the following increase: New York City 45° and 59° F., Omaha 41° and 60° F., Denver 37° and 63° F., Yuma 58° and 86° F. The range of temperature for the months of June and July, while the ants are rearing their broods, shows similar differences: for New York 15—16°, Omaha 19°, Denver 27—28°, Yuma 29—33°. The mean annual temperatures for these localities are: New York City 52°, Omaha 50°, Denver 50°, Yuma 72°. While we should, perhaps, expect to find mounds and domes in the North Atlantic States where there is the least amount of sunlight, we see that the mean annual temperature is higher here and the diurnal fluctuation of temperature both for the breeding months and for the year is less than it is in the middle west and Rocky Mountains, so that special appliances for accelerating the growth of the brood appear to be unnecessary. But in the Middle West and especially in the Rocky Mountains it is necessary to utilize all the diurnal heat to compensate for the low nocturnal temperature and its inhibitory effects on the growth of the young. Hence the great development of mounds and domes in the mountains of Wyoming, Colorado

---

[1]) Ameisennester "Boussole du Montagnard". Naturwiss. Wochenschr. N. F. VI, 1907, pp. 391, 392, 1 fig.

[2]) Climatology of the United States. U. S. Dep. Agri. Weather Bureau. Bull. 2, Washington D. C.

and New Mexico. And although the diurnal and annual fluctuation of temperature in the deserts of the Southwest is very great, the minimum temperatures are very high and nearly at the optimum for the ants' activities and development. Hence mounds and domes are quite superfluous in these regions and we find the colonies only under stones or in crater nests. The conditions in the South Atlantic and Pacific States are like those in the Southwest and, of course, in sandy, xerophytic regions like the pine barrens of the Central Atlantic States the conditions resemble those of the deserts.

In Europe, at least in the northern and central portions, the annual percentage of sunshine must be much less than in the corresponding parts of North America, and probably for this reason and notwithstanding the fact that the mean annual temperature differs but little from that of the North Atlantic States and the extremes are much less, dome and mounds nests are necessary for the development of many species. In xerothermic regions, however, like the southern slopes of the Alps (Canton Ticino) and certain insular spots further north (Petit Salève near Geneva, a few hill slopes at Vaud, Fully, etc.) we find the ants living under stones or making crater nests.

Where the conditions on the two continents are identical, as in moist, shady woods, we find the corresponding species or subspecies of ants living in precisely the same way under stones or in old logs or stumps. This is true of *Ponera coarctata*, *Myrmecina graminicola* and *Stenamma westwoodi* and the corresponding American forms: *P. pennsylvanica*, *M. americana*, *S. brevicorne* and *nearcticum*. The American forms, however, are more abundant, probably because our forests are in a more primitive and less disturbed condition. I succeeded nevertheless in finding many fine colonies of *P. coarctata* with larvæ and pupæ in the chestnut groves about Lugano and on Monte Ceneri, a few colonies of *M. graminicola* near Chigny and Lugano and some stray workers of *S. westwoodi* in a forest near Professor Forel's present residence at Yvorne. These species and their subspecies, as the oldest and most stable portion of the holarctic ant-fauna, range from England to Japan and from British Columbia to the North Atlantic States. To this old fauna, which probably dates from the Mesozoic, belong also the European and North American species of *Strumigenys*, *Stigmatomma*, and *Sysphincta*, and the American *Proceratium*.

IV. Notes on the Parasitic Ants of Europe.

Several authors have maintained that in Europe the fauna and flora show signs of being in a more advanced stage of evolution than in North America. No one has expressed this opinion more emphatically than Simroth[1] in his recent extraordinary application of Reibisch's theory of pendulation[2] to the geographical distribution of animals. The North American fauna and flora undoubtedly contain a greater number of archaic and conservative elements than the European (Urodela, Ganoidea among animals, *Wellingtonia*, *Liriodendron*, *Sassafras* among plants), but the total number of forms is greater and there are also several groups of plants like *Aster*, *Solidago* and *Cratægus* which are generally admitted to be in an active

---

[1] Die Pendulationstheorie. Leipzig, K. Grethlein, 1907.

[2] Ein Gestaltungsprinzip der Erde. 27. Jahresb. Ver. f. Erdkunde z. Dresden, 1901, pp. 105—124, II ibid. 1905, pp. 39—53, 2 maps.

stage of speciation. This is also probably true of the ant genera *Cremastogaster*, *Myrmica*, *Aphænogaster* and *Formica*. I can find nothing to indicate that the European have taken any steps in advance of the North American ants, with the exception of certain parasitic species among which the Old World forms show indications of greater degeneration and this, of course, implies greater phylogenetic changes. These indications are mentioned in the following notes, which, however, consist very largely of miscellaneous observations.

1. Temporary Social Parasites. — In several papers[1]), I have shown that the recently fertilized females of our North American ants of the *Formica rufa* and *exsecta* groups (*F. difficilis*, *consocians*, *dakotensis*, *microgyna*, *exsectoides*, etc.) are adopted by weak colonies of ants belonging to the *F. fusca* and *pallide-fulva* groups (*F. subsericea*, *schaufussi*, *incerta*) and have their first brood of workers brought up by these hosts. Eventually the host ants die off and a pure colony of the temporary parasite remains. I predicted that the European forms allied to *rufa* and *exsecta* would be found to have similar habits, because Forel (Fourmis de la Suisse, pp. 371—373) had previously seen small colonies of *F. truncicola*, *pratensis*, *exsecta* and *exsecto-pressilabris* mixed with *fusca*. Wasmann[2]) then showed that these forms fulfilled my predictions since their queens establish their colonies with the aid of *fusca* workers, and Santschi[3]) has recently discovered that a Dolichoderine ant, *Bothriomyrmex meridionalis*, is a temporary parasite of *Tapinoma erraticum*.

During the summer of 1907 I searched very diligently for incipient mixed colonies of the European ants above mentioned but found only a single example, which was much like the colonies described by Forel. July 1, I found on the slopes of Monte Generoso a young *F. exsecto-pressilabris* colony occupying a single small nest intermediate in size and structure between the nests of *exsecta* and *pressilabris*, and containing workers of *F. fusca*. These were about one fourth as numerous as the workers of *exsecto-pressilabris*. I failed to find the small queen of the latter species. Although I saw a great many nests of *F. rufa*, *pratensis* and *truncicola* in many localities, I could find no young colonies. Both these forms and *F. exsecta* and *pressilabris* are sporadic like their North American allies. At Vaud I had the pleasure of seeing the huge *pratensis* nest which Forel has had under observation

---

[1]) A New Type of Social Parasitism among Ants. Bull. Amer. Mus. Nat. Hist., XX, 1904, pp. 347—375; Social Parasitism Among Ants. Amer. Mus. Journ. IV, 1904, pp. 74—75; An Interpretation of the Slave-making Instincts in Ants. Bull. Amer. Mus. Nat. Hist., XXI, 1905, pp. 1—16; How the Queens of the Parasitic and Slavemaking Ants Establish their Colonies. Amer. Mus. Journ. V, 1905, pp. 144—148; Some Remarks on Temporary Social Parasitism and the Phylogeny of Slavery Among Ants. Biol. Centralbl. XXV, 1905, pp. 637—644; On the Founding of Colonies by Queen Ants, with special reference to the Parasitic and Slave-making Species. Bull. Amer. Mus. Nat. Hist. XXII, 1906, pp. 33—105, 7 pll.; The Origin of Slavery Among Ants. Pop. Sci. Monthly, 1907, pp. 550—559. The Ants of Casco Bay, Maine, with Observations on two Races of Formica sanguinea Latreille. Bull. Amer. Mus. Nat. Hist. XXIV, 1908.

[2]) Ursprung und Entwicklung der Sklaverei bei den Ameisen. Biol. Centralbl. XXV, 1905, pp. 117—127, 129—144, 161—169, 256—270, 273—292, 2 figg. Weitere Beiträge zum sozialen Parasitismus und der Sklaverei bei den Ameisen. Biol. Centralbl. XXVIII, 1908, pp. 257—271, 290—306, 321—333, 353—382, 417—441; 3 figg.

[3]) A propos des Moeurs parasitiques temporaires des Fourmis du Genre Bothriomyrmex. Ann. Soc. Entom. France, LXXV, 1906, pp. 363—392.

for the past forty years. The colony inhabiting this nest has had a succession of queens during this period, showing that the colonies of these temporary parasites, when once established, may perpetuate themselves by adopting females of their own species and thus attain an extraordinary age. Just as Professor Forel and I approached the nest at about 10 A. M. on June 5, the males and winged females were leaving it for their nuptial flight.

I found *Bothriomyrmex septentrionalis* only once, on the Petit Salève, near Geneva, in the very spot where Forel had seen it nearly forty years ago. Here there was a single large colony under a stone on a slope where colonies of *Tapinoma erraticum* abounded. The relative frequency of the two species was much like that of the temporary parasite *F. consocians* and its host *F. incerta* on the hill-slopes of Connecticut.

2. *Formica sanguinea*. — This facultative slave-maker seems to be much more abundant in Europe than are its various subspecies and varieties in North America. As Forel has shown, some of the latter forms are smaller and feebler than their Old World prototype, but make more slaves, and I may also add, have more concealed nests. I had an excellent opportunity to study *sanguinea* in Switzerland, Bavaria and Saxony. In Canton Vaud the slaves were *F. fusca* var. *glebaria* and var. *rubescens* (often mixed in the same colony) and *F. rufibarbis*. At higher altitudes and latitudes the typical *fusca* is the most frequent slave; at Sierre in the valley of the Rhone I also found *cinerea* acting in this capacity. According to Wasmann[1]), the average ratio of the European *sanguinea* workers to slaves is 3—5 : 1 and my own observations would tend to confirm this estimate. In 70 colonies of our American forms on which I have made notes the ratio of *sanguinea* to slaves is 1.5 : 4.5 which is practically the reverse of the ratio in the European forms. In both continents slaveless or nearly slaveless colonies occur. Forel observed a number of these at Maloja at the end of the Engadin, and near the same place (at Samaden and St. Moritz) I found two large areas covered with *sanguinea* nests in which the proportion of slaveless to slave-containing colonies must have been fully as 40 : 1. This is the reverse of the conditions observed by Wasmann for 410 *sanguinea* colonies in Holland. The tactics of this ant in procuring its slaves have been vividly described by Huber, Forel and Wasmann, and although I witnessed several forays I have nothing to add to the observations of these authors.

The question arises as to whether the European or American forms of *sanguinea* represent the more primitive conditions. As several of the American forms have more more decided slave-making instincts they might be regarded as the more highly specialized, but it is quite as probable that the European form may be slowly abandoning dulosis and reverting to an independent and slaveless condition. It is impossible to decide between these alternatives without a more exhaustive study of the ethology of *sanguinea* throughout its range in temperate Europe, Asia and North America.

3. *Polyergus rufescens*. — During June 1907 many fine colonies of this ant were seen in the Cantons of Vaud, Vallais and Ticino but it was too early in the year for their slave-making forays. In all cases the slaves were, as Forel has shown,

---

[1]) Die zusammengesetzten Nester und gemischten Kolonien der Ameisen. Münster, Aschendorffsche Buchdruckerei, 1891.

either the true *fusca*, its varieties *glebaria* and *rubescens*, or *rufibarbis*. There is some evidence that *Polyergus* may have slaves of different species at different times. Professor Forel showed me near Morges, a colony of this ant, which in 1904 contained only *rufibarbis* slaves, but during 1907 had *glebaria* instead. The only expedition of *Polyergus* which I witnessed was near Würzburg (July 17). At 4.30 P. M. Professor Spemann and I came upon a troop of about 100 *Polyergus* workers which were just leaving a large *rufibarbis* nest on the side of a road. The troop, laden with cocoons and larvæ, hurriedly crossed the road, then climbed over a low wall and descended into a field to a spot about 20 m. away where the nest was located. This contained many *rufibarbis* slaves of much smaller size than those from which the ants had been robbing the cocoons. Returning to the plundered colony I found the *rufibarbis* assembled on the nest or clinging to the grass blades, holding in their jaws a few larvæ and pupæ which they had saved. They vastly outnumbered the troop of *Polyergus*, but though belonging to an aggressive and ill-tempered species,

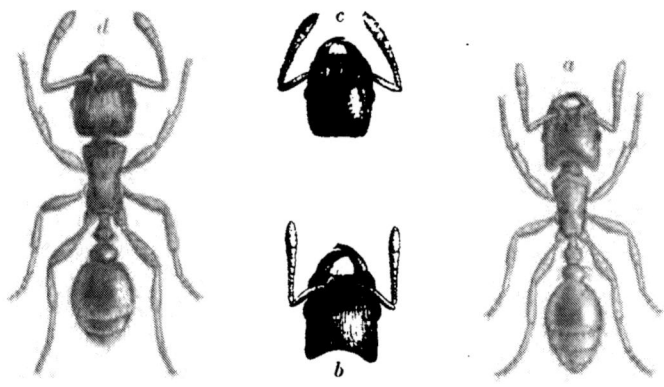

Fig. B. *Strongylognathus testaceus* Schenk, worker; *b*, head of female of same; *c*, *S. huberi* Forel, head of worker; *d*, *Tetramorium cæspitum* L. host of *S. testaceus* and *huberi*.

they had not stood their ground during the mêlée. They were, in fact, too much discouraged to bite my hand when I thrust it into their midst.

P. breviceps of the Western United States is very closely allied to the European *rufescens*. Its slaves are also forms of *fusca* whereas *P. lucidus* of the Eastern States enslaves *F. schaufussi* and forms much smaller colonies. In general, the habits of these two forms of *Polyergus* and of *P. bicolor* of Wisconsin and Illinois are very similar to those of the European type. All of these ants are of rare and local occurrence on both continents.

4. *Strongylognathus testaceus* (**Fig. B** *a* and *b*). — This parasitic ant, which belongs to a genus which is not represented in the New World, was repeatedly seen in *Tetramorium cæspitum* colonies in several localities (Vaud, Petit Salève, Monte Ceneri and Fully in Switzerland and Klotzsche near Dresden). The colonies near Klotzsche, which are especially fine, have been studied by Viehmeyer. At the time of my visit (July 25) they contained hundreds of males and winged females of *Strongylognathus*. On this ant Professor Forel and I made an observation which agrees with one made several years ago by Wasmann in Bohemia. He found a large mixed colony which contained 15 000—20 000 *Tetramorium* and some thousand *Strongylognathus* together with pupæ of both species. About 70% of the pupæ were

males and females of the parasitic species, the remainder were worker pupæ, and there were two large male pupæ of the host. This nest contained a fertile queen of *Tetramorium* and one of *Strongylognathus* living side by side. June 11, Professor Forel and I found a similar *Strongylognathus-Tetramorium* colony on the Petit Salève. This colony, though much smaller than the one described by Wasmann, contained a fertile *Tetramorium* queen. The diminutive *Strongylognathus* queen was not found but must have been present as the nest contained young worker pupæ in addition to the imagines of the parasitic species. Wasmann is inclined to believe that these mixed colonies arise through the alliance of a *Strongylognathus* and a *Tetramorium* queen, but it is more probable that the former enters a colony of the latter after it has been established and become populous, since the founding of colonies even by pairs of queens of the same species is an extremely rare occurrence[1]).

5. *Harpagoxenus sublævis*. — This parasitic species, which usually passes in the literature as *Tomognathus sublævis*, was found by Viehmeyer under stones in *Leptothorax acervorum* nests on the heaths near Dresden. He also discovered that this ant, previously supposed to be confined to boreal Europe and to have only ergatoid females, also develops winged females, at least in Saxony. On Mr. Viehmeyer's collecting grounds I had the pleasure of finding a fine colony of *Harpagoxenus* which, however, contained only ergatoid females and workers. This ant is decidedly larger than *H. americanus*, which lives with *Leptothorax curvispinosus* in hollow twigs. The American form has only winged queens, apparently, and on this account I placed it in a separate subgenus, *Protomognathus*. This must be abandoned, now that Viehmeyer has discovered similar females in the European species. Observations on both species are too meager to enable me to decide which shows the more advanced parasitism or whether they differ in this respect.

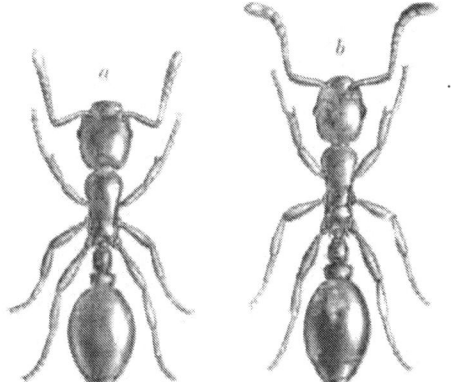

Fig. C. *Formicoxenus nitidulus* Nyl., *a*, worker; *b*, ergatomorphic male.

6. *Formicoxenus nitidulus* (**Fig. C**) is an interesting little ant that lives with *Formica rufa* and has wingless and highly ergatoid males, first discovered by Adlerz[2]). This condition makes a nuptial flight impossible, of course, so that mating has to take place on the surface of the *Formica* nest or on the ground and stones in the neighborhood. The mating has been seen by several European observers and on July 11, I had an opportunity to witness it near Samaden on the slopes of Piz Ot,

---

[1]) I have called attention to a case of this kind in the North American *Lasius brevicornis*. June 15, while collecting at Sion in Canton Vallais I found a very similar case — two deälated queens of *Lasius flavus* under a stone in a small earthen cavity a few cm. in diameter, in which they were nursing a single packet of eggs and young larvæ. Both hastened to remove the brood when the stone was lifted.

[2]) Myrmecologiska Studier. I Formicoxenus nitidulus, Nyl. Öfversigt af Kongl. Vetenskaps-Akad. Förh. VIII, pp. 43—64, Tab. 27—28.

at an altitude of about 2000 m. in the Upper Engadin. After a cold night the sun remained behind a mass of clouds till about 9 A. M. when I saw dozens of *Formicoxenus* males, females and workers, but mostly males running hither and thither over the small twigs and other débris forming the outer covering of an old *rufa* nest which I had stopped to examine. The males moved very quickly, with peculiarly curved and feverishly vibrating antennæ, and were so amorous that they often seized workers and attempted to mate with them. The comparatively few winged females were soon supplied with partners and the supernumerary males continued to hurry about over and among the little sticks of the nest. Then the sun suddenly emerged from the clouds and, as if by magic, all the *Formicoxeni* disappeared into the nest. I waited for some time and during the remainder of the morning returned repeatedly to the spot, but none of the tiny inquilines reappeared.

F. nitidulus is represented in the western United States by *Symmyrmica chamberlini* (**Fig. D**), which lives in the nests of *Myrmica mutica*. The male *Sym-*

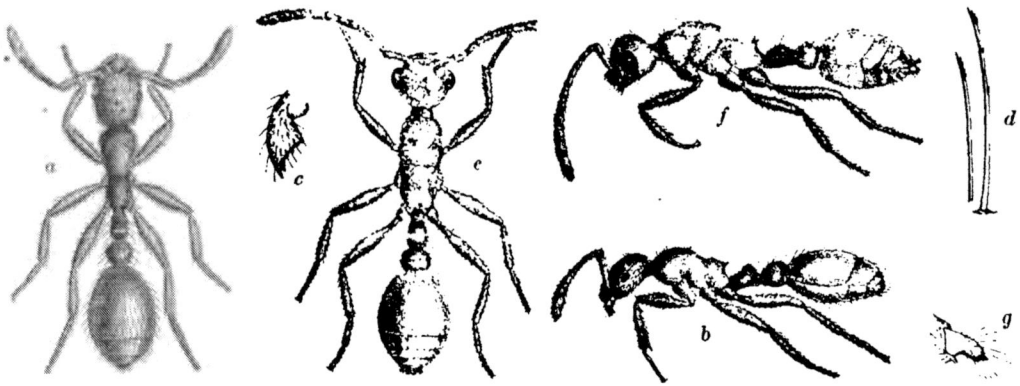

Fig. D. *Symmyrmica chamberlini* Wheeler; *a* and *b*, worker; *c*, mandible, *d*, hairs of same; *e* and *f*, ergatomorphic male; *g*, mandible of same.

myrmica is also ergatoid but less so than the male of *Formicoxenus*, and this may be taken to indicate that the American is less modified than the European form. It is not improbable that *Myrmica rubida*, which is closely related to *M. mutica*, is the original host of *Formicoxenus* and that its relations with *F. rufa* are secondary and of comparatively recent origin. Careful examination of *rubida* nests in some parts of Europe may show that the little inquiline has not completely forsaken its original host.

7. *Anergates atratulus* (**Fig. E**). — On only one occasion was I fortunate enough to find a colony of this rare, workerless parasite. June 6, at 2 P. M., while collecting near Vaud, in the very meadow in which Forel as a young man made many of his classical observations for the "Fourmis de la Suisse", I discovered a medium-sized *Tetramorium cæspitum* colony from which female *Anergates* were escaping in considerable numbers. The nest was around the roots of a plantain (*Plantago major*) and the females issued one by one from the entrances, climbed the leaves to their tips, and flew away in all directions over the sun-lit grass. At 3.30 P. M. Prof. Forel joined me and we excavated the nest with great care. It contained besides the obese mother queen of *Anergates* (Fig. E*b*) and several hundred

Tetramorium workers, more than a thousand winged queens (Fig. E*a*), a few hundred of the wingless, pupa-like males (Fig. E*d*), several pupæ and a few larvæ of the parasitic species. In the galleries of the nest dozens of couples were united in the act of mating. The *Tetramorium* workers picked up the single males and hurried away with them, but they paid little attention to the females. The colony was placed in a bag and on the following day used for experiments on *Tetramorium* colonies in Prof. Forel's garden at Chigny. On opening the bag the next morning, I found several of the *Anergates in copulâ*, but most of the females had either lost their wings or were ready to drop them at the slightest touch. Eight *Tetramorium* colonies that had large nests with multiple craters in the paths of the garden, were selected, and the females were placed near them, one at a time, on the ground. In

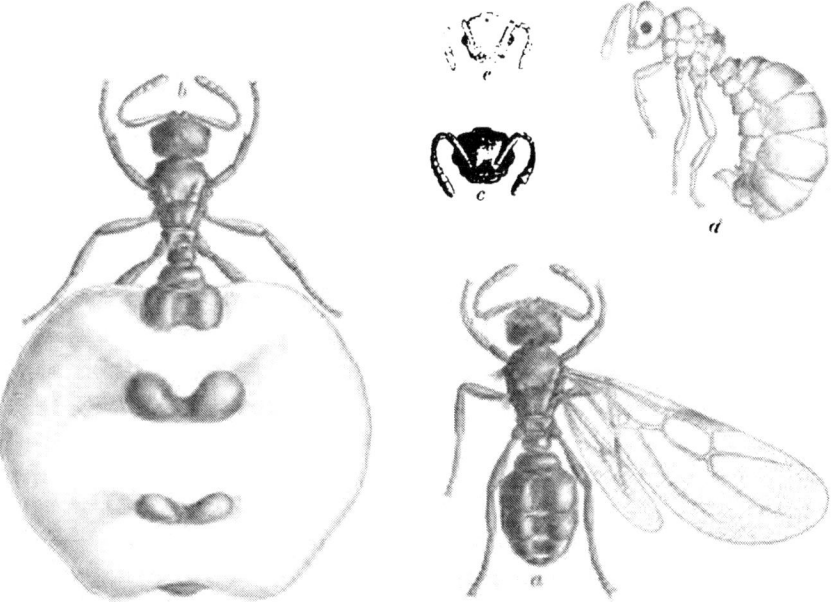

Fig. E. *Anergates atratulus* Schenk; *a*, virgin female; *b*, old queen; *c* head of same; *d*, pupoid male; *e* head of same. From specimens taken at Vaud, Switzerland.

all cases when they were placed within a few centimeters of the openings, they entered the nest almost immediately; when placed at a greater distance they wandered about demurely till they found an opening and then at once crept into it. Seven of the nests were thus entered by numbers of the queens without creating the slightest excitement among the *Tetramorium* workers. These merely stopped when they happened to meet a female, seized her by the wings, thorax or pedicel, but at once dropped her and went about their work. In no case was one of the queens injured. In three of these colonies they were seized by single workers and carried into the nest as fast as I could set them on the craters. Both males and females were placed near the openings of one of the nests. The males were seized with signs of keen interest and some animosity, to judge from the way in which the workers bent their gasters forward and tried to sting the helpless creatures. They were not killed, however, but carried a few decimeters from the nest and thrown away, sometimes from the top of a pebble or lump of earth. This was being done while other workers were carrying the females into the nest. One vigorous colony exhibited a different behavior. All the parasites, both male and female, were at once seized, pulled about by the legs, wings and antennæ and then carried away and dumped on the ground at some distance from the nest. In this instance several of the parasites of both sexes were injured so that they could not walk. Strange *Tetramorium* workers placed on any of the nests above mentioned were suddenly pounced upon and killed. These observations show that the *Anergates* queens are, as a rule, treated with great lenity and even carried into the nests, but that the males are rejected. They also show that certain colonies are positively hostile to both sexes of the parasites. In all cases, however, the behavior of the *Anergates* queens was very uniform: they sought and entered the *Tetramorium* nests as if these belonged to them, offered no resistance when seized and, when roughly handled, merely curled up and feigned death. The experiments were continued throughout the morning. With the gradually increasing temperature towards noon the *Tetramorium* workers became more numerous and active outside their nests but their treatment of the *Anergates*, which I was continually giving them, remained the same. Late in the afternoon the experiments were repeated with two of the colonies which during the morning had been entered without protest by a number of the parasitic queens. The workers were out in a multitude, excavating and dragging in insect food. When male, female or pupal *Anergates* were placed on these nests, the males and pupæ were promptly seized and thrown away and the females were also seized, but less promptly, and also rejected. Some of the latter that had managed to enter the nests were brought out and dumped at a distance of several decimeters from the entrances. I watched the nests for some time and although a few of the females were not brought out, I am, of course, unable to state whether they were subsequently adopted, killed in the galleries or ejected. It appears, therefore, that the acceptance of *Anergates* by the *Tetramorium* under natural conditions is not as immediate as the observations of Adlerz and Wasmann on artificial nests would lead one to suppose. The fact that *Anergates* is so rare an ant, although its sporadic colonies produce enormous numbers of females in regions inhabited by myriads of *Tetramorium* colonies, shows that permanent adoption is not easily effected. Were the contrary the case, *T. cæspitum* would itself become a rare, if not extinct, species[1]).

The genus *Anergates* is not represented in North America, which has instead three other genera of permanently parasitic Myrmicine ants, *Epoecus*, *Sympheidole* and *Epipheidole*, that have lost their worker caste. The males and females, however, show none of the remarkable modifications seen in *Anergates*. And although the American genera have no close phylogenetic connection with *Anergates*, they may be said nevertheless to represent a more archaic stage of permanent social parasitism.

8. *Solenopsis fugax*. — After observing this tiny yellow thief-ant in a number of localities in Switzerland and Germany, I could find little difference between its

---

[1]) Professor Forel recently wrote me that he visited the *Tetramorium* colonies at Chigny early the post summer (1908), but found that they had adopted none of the numerous *Anergates* females which Ihad given them the year before. The complete absence of the parasites was proved by the presence of male and female *Tetramorium* pupæ in all the nests. This observation, of course, merely confirms the concluding statements in the foregoing paragraph.

habits and those of the closely allied North American *S. molesta*. Both are sometimes found nesting in independent formicaries and both excavate the same kind of tenuous galleries communicating with the chambers of the other larger ants on whose larvæ and pupæ they feed. The American species is, perhaps, more versatile, as it sometimes lives in houses and is also known to resort occasionally to a vegetarian diet.

The two following conclusions may be drawn from the foregoing notes and the much larger body of observations that have been published by various authors on the symbiotic ants of Europe and North America:

1. If we except the degenerate dulosis of the *Strongylognathus* species of Europe and the peculiar xenobiosis of *Leptothorax emersoni* in America, we find that the different types of social parasitism are represented on both continents by species, subspecies or varieties which are in most cases closely related. There is, therefore, every reason to believe that these various types were developed before the separation of the continents and certainly prior to the Glacial Epoch. But as none of these parasitic forms has yet been recognized in the Tertiary we are unable to determine how far back their history extends. That *Formica sanguinea* and *Polyergus breviceps* have the same slave, or host (*F. fusca*) on both continents is, of course, additional evidence of the community of origin and the great antiquity of the two continental faunas.

2. The various types of social parasitism do not show a uniform phylogenetic development on the two continents, nor are all the types in a more advanced stage in Europe. Temporary social parasitism is more general in North America and, as shown by the minute stature of the female in several species of *Formica*, has reached a stage of greater specialization. On the other hand, the types of parasitism represented by *Formicoxenus* and *Anergates* are more highly specialized than in their American allies. *Formica sanguinea*, *Polyergus* and *Harpegoxenus* must be more carefully and extensively studied on both continents before satisfactory ethological comparisons can be instituted. *Solenopsis fugax* and *S. molest a*seem to be in a very similar stage of ethological development in their respective environments.

V. A Few Remarks on Myrmecophiles.

Just as the study of the animals and plants domesticated by human tribes has been of great service to the ethnologist in determining the migrations, cultures and contacts of these tribes, so an exhaustive study of the numerous insects that regularly live in the ant-nests of Europe and North America bids fair to throw considerable light on the geographical distribution and ethological affinities of the ants themselves. But as this study is still in its infancy, I can do little more than allude to it in the present paper. From the data that have been collected during the past twenty years by Father Wasmann, that most diligent of all students of the myrmecophiles, it is certain that many genera of these insects are represented by species on both continents, e. g. the beetles *Homœusa, Myrmedonia, Batrisus, Amphotis, Catopomorphus* and *Hetærius*, the fly *Microdon*, the cricket *Myrmecophila*, the coccid *Ripersia*, the Thyanura *Cyphodeirus* and *Atelura*, etc. In all cases, however, the species on the two continents are distinct. Other genera are closely allied. Thus the Eurasian beetle genera *Lomechusa* and *Atemeles* are represented by *Xenodusa* in North America, *Claviger* by *Adranes*, *Cetonia* by *Euphoria*, *Clytra* by *Coscinoptera*. Often, too, we find that the allied myrmecophiles of the two continents live with allied species, subspecies or varieties of ants. There are, however, many genera that are peculiar to one of the continents, e. g. *Cremastochilus*, a group of singular Scarabæid beetles, which are confined to North America, though their normal hosts are species of the circumpolar genus *Formica*.

Unquestionably the most interesting of the European myrmecophiles are the species of *Lomechusa* and *Atemeles*. Wasmann has described the life history of *Lomechusa strumosa* (**Fig. F**) in a long series of articles[1]) and has shown that its presence in colonies of *Formica sanguinea* leads to the development of pseudogynes, or pathological individuals intermediate in structure between the queens and workers. Similar forms are produced in colonies of the American *F. rubicunda* and *incerta* by the allied *Xenodusa cava* as has been shown by Muckermann[2]) and myself[3]).

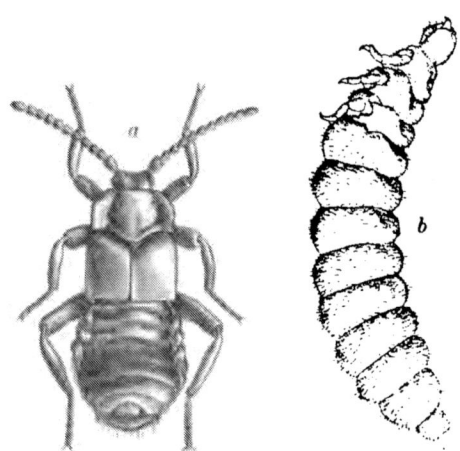

Fig. F. *Lomechusa strumosa* Jab.; *a*, imaginal beetle; *b*, full-grown larva.

The beetles of the genera *Lomechusa* and *Atemeles* are far more abundant in Europe than are those of the genus *Xenodusa* in America. At Samaden and St. Moritz in the Upper Engadin I had an excellent opportunity to observe *L. strumosa* (July 8 and 9) in the mostly slaveless colonies of *Formica sanguinea* mentioned. These colonies often contained hundreds of *Lomechusa* larvæ in all stages of growth and distributed in little clusters among the ant-brood on which they feed. When the nests were disturbed the ants often removed the parasites in preference to their own young. Several beetles were also seen in the nests. The colonies infested with the beetle larvæ were all large and flourishing and contained very few or no pseudogynes, but in the same localities there were several small and greatly impoverished communities comprising a high percentage of these abnormal individuals, but no larvæ and few beetles. Curiously enough, these degenerate and obviously moribund colonies were all found under small stones in low, damp ground, whereas the large and flourishing, and evidently only recently infected colonies, with abundant brood of both ants and beetles, were in old stumps on higher and dryer ground. A study of these colonies would convince the most skeptical of the truth of Was-

---

[1]) For a list of these articles see Wasmann's Neue Bestätigungen der Lomechusa-Pseudogynen-Theorie. Verhand. deutsch. zool. Ges., 1902, pp. 107—108.

[2]) Formica sanguinea subsp. rubicunda Em. and Xenodusa cava Lec. Entom. News, Dec. 1904, pp. 339—341, pl. XX.

[3]) The Polymorphism of Ants, with an Account of Some Singular Abnormalities Due to Parasitism. Bull. Amer. Mus. Nat. Hist. XXIII, 1907, pp. 1—93, pll. I—VI.

mann's "Lomechusa-pseudogyne theory", if this had not been more satisfactorily demonstrated by the experiments of Viehmeyer[1]).

There is only one other observation on myrmecophiles which I find worth recording. In the neighborhood of Würzburg I came upon a colony of *Formica sanguinea* in the act of moving to a new nest. The ants, laden with their larvæ and pupæ, were marching along a dusty road and in the midst of their ranks were two specimens of the Staphylinid beetle *Dinarda dentata*, accompanying their hosts to the new nest.

Explanation of the Plates.
Plate III.

Fig. 1. Nest of *Formica rufa integra* Nyl. in a log, the openings of which are stuffed with vegetable detritus by the ants. Colebrook, Connecticut.

Fig. 2. Nest of *Formica rufa integra* var. *hæmorrhoidalis* Emery, built about an old pine stump. Florissant, Colorado.

Fig. 3. Mound nest of *Formica rufa* L. Belgium. From a photograph by G. Severin.

Fig. 4. Mound nest of *Formica rufa obscuripes* Forel, resembling the nest of European *F. pratensis*, Florissant, Colorado.

Fig. 5. Nest (modified and enlarged masonry dome) of *Formica exsectoides* Forel. Scotch Plains, New Jersey.

Plate IV.

Fig. 6. Nest (modified and enlarged crater) of *Pogonomyrmex occidentalis* Cresson, surrounded by a circular clearing, in an *Artemisia frigida* formation. Maniton, Colorado.

Fig. 8. Crater of *Pogonomyrmex comanche* Wheeler, in pure sand. Austin, Texas.

Fig. 9. Disc (vestigial crater) of *Pogonomyrmex barbatus rugosus* Emery, showing to the right one of the paths, worn through the vegetation by the ants. Tucson, Arizona.

Fig. 10. Gravel crater of *Myrmecocystus mexicanus* Wesm. var. *horti-deorum* McCook. Maniton, Colorado.

---

[1]) Experimente zu Wasmanns Lomechusa-Pseudogynen-Theorie. Allgem. Zeitschr. f. Entom. IX, 1904, pp. 334—344.

Journal f. Psychol. u. Neurol. Bd. XIII.
(Wheeler, Comparative Ethology of Ants)

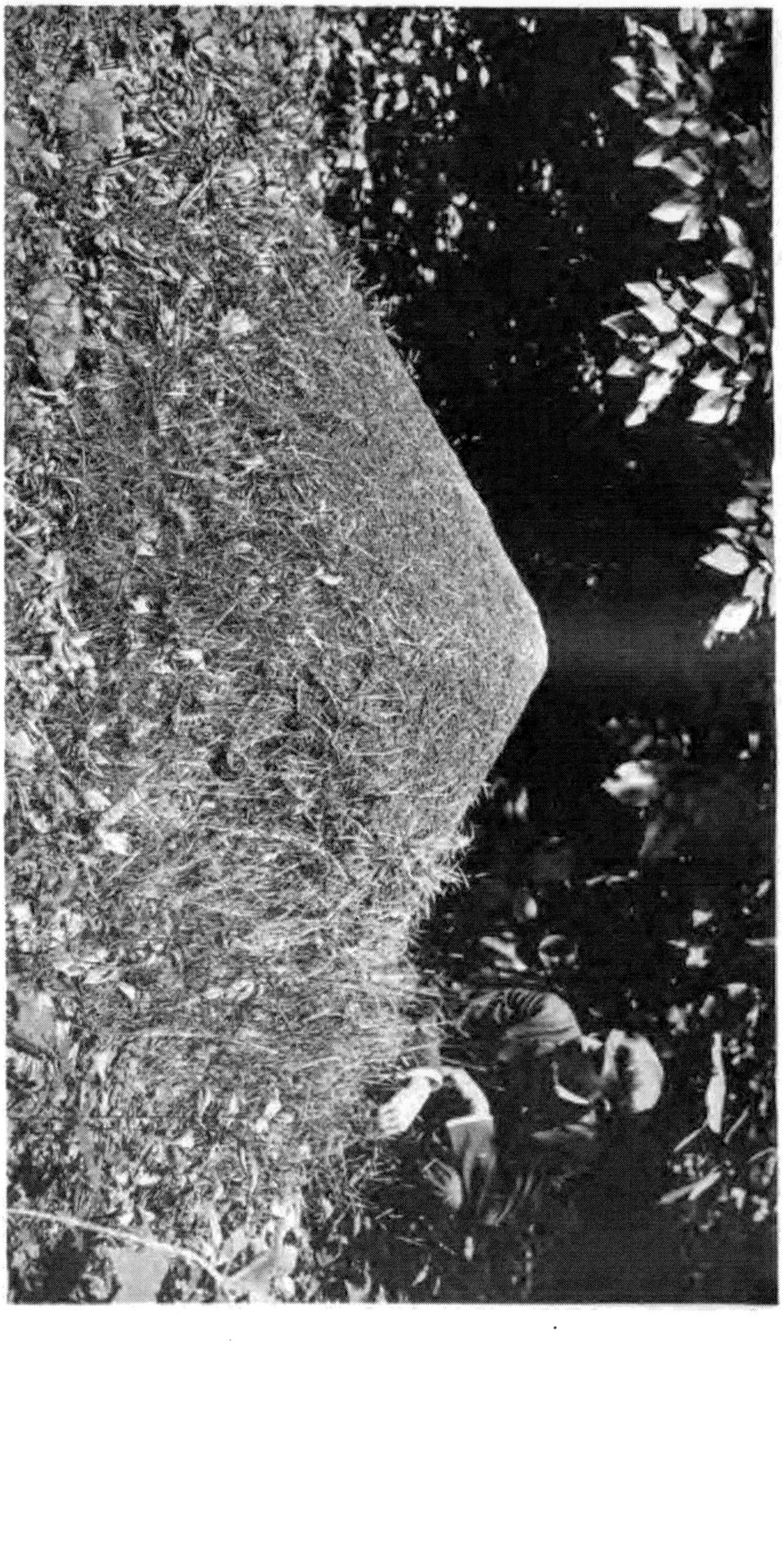

5

3

4

Tafel 3.

1

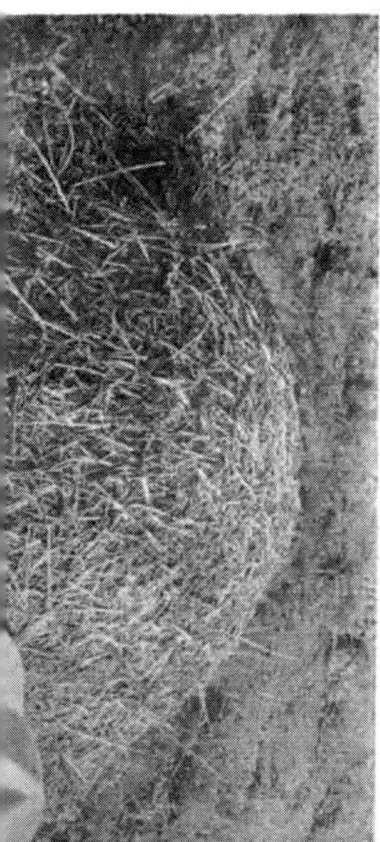

2

Lichtdruck von Albert Frisch, Berlin W 85.

Journal f. Psychol. u. Neurol. Bd. XIII.
(Wheeler, Comparative Ethology of Ants.)

6

9

Tafel 4.

8

10

Lichtdruck von Albert Frisch, Berlin W 35.

Printed by Libri Plureos GmbH in Hamburg, Germany